1 MONTH OF FREE READING

at

www.ForgottenBooks.com

By purchasing this book you are eligible for one month membership to ForgottenBooks.com, giving you unlimited access to our entire collection of over 1,000,000 titles via our web site and mobile apps.

To claim your free month visit:
www.forgottenbooks.com/free953207

* Offer is valid for 45 days from date of purchase. Terms and conditions apply.

ISBN 978-0-260-51402-8
PIBN 10953207

This book is a reproduction of an important historical work. Forgotten Books uses state-of-the-art technology to digitally reconstruct the work, preserving the original format whilst repairing imperfections present in the aged copy. In rare cases, an imperfection in the original, such as a blemish or missing page, may be replicated in our edition. We do, however, repair the vast majority of imperfections successfully; any imperfections that remain are intentionally left to preserve the state of such historical works.

Forgotten Books is a registered trademark of FB &c Ltd.
Copyright © 2018 FB &c Ltd.
FB &c Ltd, Dalton House, 60 Windsor Avenue, London, SW19 2RR.
Company number 08720141. Registered in England and Wales.

For support please visit www.forgottenbooks.com

Ontario Provincial Liberal Party
     Finance, agriculture, government
House, 1919.

Ontario Provincial Liberal Party

Finance

Agriculture

Government House

1919

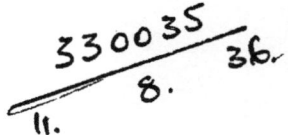

For Additional Copies, Apply to

W. H. ADAMS, General Secretary

36 TORONTO ST.   TORONTO

FINANCE

Public Accounts a Chinese Puzzle.

Time and again the Liberals in the House have urged a clearer statement of the financial affairs of the Province. The Public Accounts seem to be compiled with the express object of puzzling the ordinary citizen or the representatives of the people in Parliament. During the last session of the Legislature (1919) the Liberals protested by resolution against the concealment of specific and important items of current receipts under the heading of "Casual Revenue". Entries were made in the Public Accounts of revenue from work done by tractors, sale of seed wheat and the Dominion grant for food production for the fiscal year 1917-18 under this heading, when they should have been made under the heading of "Agriculture". The Liberals also protested against receipts from the disposal of capital assets, such as timber, being treated as current receipts instead of receipts on capital account while payments were treated as capital payments.

Year after year the Liberal Opposition has appealed against the unwarranted expenditure in connection with Government House and the exorbitant cost of civil government generally.

The following is a copy of the resolution which the Government defeated in 1919:—

"This House disapproves of and protests against (1) the presentation to this House by the Honourable the Provincial Treasurer of financial statements which do not fairly set forth the real character of the financial transactions of the Government; (2) the extravagant and wasteful expenditure of public money by the Government, as illustrated by the annual expenditure on maintenance of the Government House, when important public services such as Education, Agriculture and Roads are in great need of further funds; (3) the concealment of specific and important items of current receipts in respect of any department under the heading of "Casual Revenue", as illustrated by the entries made of revenue from work done by tractors, sale of seed wheat and the Dominion grant for food production, in the statement for 1917-18; (4) the treatment of receipts from the disposal of capital assets such as timber, as current receipts, while at the same time treating the payments as on capital account when it is apparent from their nature they should be disbursed as payment out of current revenue; (5) the exorbitant cost of civil government at the present time."

Mr. C. M. Bowman, Liberal member for West Bruce, in the Budget Debate pointed out that while the total expenditure during the year 1918 in connection with the war amounted to about $3,600,000, the Public Accounts disclosed that under the item of "Casual Revenue", which is treated as a current receipt there was received from the sale of tractors and the sale of seed wheat and from the grant received from the Dominion Government in connection with greater food production, the sum of $60,000, showing a total receipt of $378,321.09 which was treated as current receipt and not taken into consideration by the Treasurer in connection with war expenditure.

In considering the receipts and expenditure relating to Northern Ontario Mr. Bowman brought to the attention of the House the receipt by the Crown Lands Department as bonuses on timber the sum of $679,304.17 and from timber dues $790,-604.08 or a total of $1,475,908.25, and that this had been treated as a current receipt. He explained that this money came into the hands of the Treasurer through the disposal of capital assets of the province and that therefore the capital assets of the province were reduced in value by that amount. He strongly objected to treating receipts of that nature as current receipts.

Comparing the cost of civil government in 1906 with the cost during the past year, Mr. Bowman showed an increase from $428,208,46, to $1,013,721.54, or 136%.

Estimates.

The estimates of the present Government, large as they are, are always a long way removed from the actual receipts and expenditures. In his budget speech of 1918 the Provincial Treasurer estimated the ordinary receipts for the coming year at $17,044.728 and the expenditure at $11,570,533.82. He received $19,270,123.71 and spent $17,460,404.05, or about 6 millions more than he led the House and the country to believe would be expended during that year. It is absolutely impossible to rely upon the statements of the Government relating to its financial operations with any degree of certainty. They would do discredit to any well conducted business house.

The Estimated Expenditure for the Current Year.

Last year the estimated expenditure was roughly 11 millions and the actual expenditure 17 millions. This year the estimated expenditure is roughly placed at 15 millions. Judging by past experience this would mean an actual expenditure of 21 millions, for what, we do not know, for the Government does not itself know. The object of the estimates is to indicate to the people how their money is spent. The object of the Government seems to be to spend the money according to its own will without taking the people into its confidence as to how the money is expended until after the expenditure is made.

A comparison between expenditure in the last year of the Liberal regime and the current year shows an increase that is absolutely appalling. The total expenditure for the year 1904, when the Liberals were in power, as shown by the Public Accounts was $5,267,453; the total expenditure for the year 1918, with the present Government in power, was $17,460,404.

Statutory Expenditure.

The statutory expenditure in 1918 was $14,442,203.74; it will almost certainly exceed this amount for the present year. If we add to the estimated ordinary expenditure of $15,000,000 a further sum of $6,000,000 by which the estimates were exceeded last year, and at the same time include a like amount for 1919 for statutory expenditure as was paid out in 1918, the Province will face this year the enormous expenditure of $21,000,000 ordinary expenditure and $14,000,000 at least statutory expenditure, or $35,000,000!

Expenditure per Head of the Population.

At the end of the first financial year in 1867 the ordinary payments amounted to only $554,623.70. In 1871 they had risen to $1,629,250.22; but this represented a payment of only $1.00 per head of the population according to the Dominion census of that year. If we take the census statistics of 1901—toward the end of the Liberal regime—and compare with the expenditure, we find that the payment per head was only $1.63 upon an expenditure of $3,558,635.78. Upon the 1911 statistics, with the Conservatives in power, the payment had risen to nearly $3.00 per head and the expenditure had amounted to $7,445,617.64; Last year (1918), with an expenditure of $17,460,404.15, allowing for an item of $2,054,212 in connection with the war and an item of $4,277,934 for public buildings—which were not included in ordinary expenditure in the earlier accounts—bringing the amount of expenditure down to $11,128,257.21, and taking the official census figures for Ontario of 1911 at 2,523,274, the expenditure now amounts to the outrageous sum of $4.41 per head!

A comparison of a few items will indicate how this enormous increase is made up:—

Cost of Civil Government.

1919 (estimate by Treasurer)	$1,163,700.00
1904	344,000.00
Increase	819,700.00

Legislation.

1919 (estimates)	328,700.00
1904	200,000.00
Increase	128,700.00

Administration of Justice.

1919 (estimates)	797,860.00
1904	482,000.00
Increase	315,860.00

The Public Debt.

The increase in the public debt since 1904 is even more striking. The Public Debt, or direct liabilities of the Province, amounted during the financial year 1917-18 to over $75,000,000. In 1904 it was only $11,709,651.

Compare the years—

1904	$11,709,651
1908	17,282,592
1911	24,765,923
1914	49,389,366
1918	75,645,917

The reckless extravagance of the Government has never been condoned by the Liberal Opposition. Despite the most vigorous protests the Government has relied upon its docile majority in the House to sanction any expenditure that it undertook. The Liberal policy, on the other hand, has always been to ascertain:—

(1) Whether the borrowing and expenditure were necessary for the proper development of the Province.

(2) Whether the Government was getting a dollar in value for every dollar expended.

The Consolidated Revenue Fund.

After the estimates, supplementary and further supplementary estimates have been passed, the same are incorporated in an Act for granting to His Majesty certain sums of money for the Public Service of the current financial year and the ensuing one. It is always enacted that these sums shall be paid out of the Consolidated Revenue Fund of the Province, which is the accumulation of ordinary receipts over ordinary expenditure, excluding transactions chargeable to Capital or of a statutory nature. All money raised by way of loan for the public service is also secured upon the credit of this fund and in the last analysis is chargeable thereto.

Up to the year 1906 (the year after the Conservative Administration came into power) the Public Accounts contained a statement of the Consolidated Revenue Account, to which was added each year the excess of receipts on ordinary account over expenditure, and the public was able to tell at a glance the strength of the Consolidated Revenue of the Province, upon which appropriations have to be made and upon the credit of which loans are secured for the carrying out of all kinds of public works and the liquidation of floating debts. This Account was discontinued by the Conservatives in the year 1907, and the consequence is that members of the House have to deduct from the total receipts and expenditures whatever they consider belongs to Capital Account, in order to ascertain the ordinary receipts and expenditures which are chargeable to the Consolidated Revenue Fund; and even then they have no means of determining what the Consolidated Revenue Fund of Ontario now amounts to, because since 1907 there has been no statement in the Public Accounts showing the position of this Account. The present Government takes care to boost the estimated resources of the Province. They estimate them at $600,000,000, but the public must remember that it is not against the resources of the Province that money is appropriated or loans secured, but upon the credit of the Consolidated Revenue Fund, which no one can at present ascertain from the Public Accounts tabled in the Legislature.

Commissions.

One of the most striking charges against the present Administration is that it is governed by Commissions at a tremendous expense of public money, instead of performing the functions of government itself. This Commission Government has failed to realise that the people of Ontario do not pay salaries to Ministers of the Crown and provide them with large staffs merely to dispose of the public monies by creating expensive commissions. The Government repeatedly declined to appoint a most necessary commission to investigate the depopulation of rural Ontario demanded by the Liberals in the House for years and conceded on the public platform to be in line with what the farming community believes to be the solution of the problem. A comparison of expenditure in respect of Commissions, however, before and after the present Government was elected to office shows how the Conservative Government unnecessarily delegates its duties to others. From 1872 to 1905 (for which years the Liberal Party must be held responsible) expenditures on Commissions, as appears by the Public Accounts, amounted to only $269,696.19. Subsequent to 1905, during the Conservative regime up to 1917, the huge amount of $2,216,699.80 has been handed out to various Commissions and Boards, or 82 times as much in a period of 12 years as the Liberal Party found it necessary to spend in 33 years. Some of the Commissions were necessary, but in other cases the appointment of a Commission was only an expedient to delay action and an attempt to allay public discontent, as is instanced in the Nickel Report which cost $85,474.11, the Unemployment Report which cost exactly $8,000,00, and the Roads Commission dealing with Township Roads which cost $6,000.00 and has not been acted upon.

The Annual Surplus.

The Provincial Treasurer always endeavours to show a surplus of ordinary receipts over expenditure in his financial statement; and reviewing the fiscal year 1917-18 at the ensuing session of the Legislature, he claimed a surplus of $1,809,719. If, however, capital receipts were always credited to capital account instead of to current receipts the figures would tell quite a different story. When the statement of receipts and expenditures is carefully examined it is quite apparent that nothing in that statement makes such a *revenue surplus* possible. The dance of figures where so many financial operations cross one another during the year, many of them incomplete, affords the opportunity for clever financial gymnastics.

One of the credit items to the Department of Lands, Forests & Mines is a profit tax of $863,000. The Liberals objected that the accounts should show details of the source from which this total sum was realised. If the details had been given we should have known how much of this profit tax came from the Canadian Copper Co. (the Canadian name for the International Nickel Co.) In view of the fact that the pressure of the Liberal Opposition resulted in the recovery for the country of $1,360,000 for two years' taxes from this company, instead of the $80,000 the Government had illegally accepted, one may easily estimate the nickel tax that was included in the general profit tax at the sum of $600,000, for the recovery of which the Liberal Opposition and not the Government is entitled to credit.

Similarly, it is interesting to note that in the revenue for the year 1917-18 the succession duty tax yielded $3,157,000. The income from the same source during the last year of the Liberal administration in 1904 was only $450,000. It is rather amusing to have the Government claim credit for a surplus that would not have existed if Providence had not seen fit to take a few of our rich men to himself. But for the act of Providence, the Provincial Treasurer would have had to apologise for an unexpected deficit instead of taking credit for a surplus to which an act of the Government is supposed to have contributed.

Taxation.

One of the resolutions unanimously passed by the recent Provincial Liberal Convention held at Toronto, was as follows:—

> "That this Convention favours local option for municipalities to assess and tax improvements, including buildings, business and income, on a lower basis than land, and that the Liberal principle of raising as much as possible of the Provincial revenues by the taxation of natural resources be hereby affirmed."

This has been the settled policy of the Provincial Liberal Party for years. In the platform of the party in 1911, the principle of Local Option in Taxation was set forth. It was pointed out that the present system under which taxation is levied for municipal purposes has caused profound discontent in the great cities and in New Ontario. In the cities it has been the means of encouraging land speculation, whereby one person improves his property and pays taxes for the benefit of adjoining vacant lots; and in New Ontario speculators are holding unimproved locations until the actual settlers open up the country.

The Liberal platform provides that each municipality shall be given the right to so adjust its system of taxation as to remove grievances such as these, and to depend upon the taxation of our natural resources for the bulk of provincial revenues.

AGRICULTURE

The Liberal Policy.

(Adopted at the Provincial Liberal Convention).

Moved by Nelson Parliament, M.P.P., seconded by J. A. Calder, M.P.P., "Recognizing the important position occupied by the agricultural industry, and the difficulties which confront it, be it resolved:

1. A system of rural credits be established to provide long term money at a low rate of interest.

2. That agricultural schools with demonstration farms be established to continue the education of rural and urban boys and girls after leaving the public school.

3. That the spirit of co-operation between producer and consumer be encouraged with a view to cheapening the cost of production as well as that of distribution."

The Liberal Party recognizes the important position occupied by the industry of Agriculture and the difficulties which confront it. It also recognises the absolute failure of the Government to effectively meet these conditions. The cardinal principles of the Liberal Party are:—

(1) Efficient leadership and effective administration by a Minister whose practical experience enables him to give leadership in agricultural matters.

(2) Having regard to the serious decline in rural population, a thorough survey and inquiry by a non-partizan commission of practical men into the conditions of agriculture and rural life in Ontario.

(3) The establishment of Agricultural schools and Demonstration Farms throughout the Province.

(4) The inauguration of an effective system of rural credits.

(5) The development of co-operative effort in buying and selling.

(6) Financial assistance by way of loans at a low rate of interest on the security of lands and improvements to assist settlers.

(7) The acquiring by the Government of farms in Older Ontario for the purpose of settling returned soldiers, with proper assistance.

There have been ample evidences within the last few years that the existing spirit of unrest and dissatisfaction has extended to the agricultural classes. The reasons are not far to seek. Not only does the farmer consider that he was treated unjustly and in bad faith by the Government at Ottawa, but he considers that his interests have been neglected by the Government in Ontario from their failure to realize the real needs of the community and to apply such remedies as would have stimulated Agriculture and attracted men to the land.

A study of the history of the treatment of the agricultural interests of Ontario will show that they were fostered and made progress under a Liberal Administration while they have declined under the present Government.

In striking contrast to Hon. John Dryden, who put the Department of Agriculture in Ontario on a plane of effective usefulness, the late Hon. James Duff let the department sink into a position of second rate importance. Under him the Department lacked initiative and progressiveness.

It was not only Liberals who criticized the Department of Agriculture as administered by Hon. James Duff. Sir Jos. Flavelle then Mr. J. W. Flavelle, one of the leading Conservatives in the Province, wrote a letter to Mr. Duff in which occurred the following criticism.

> "You have permitted, you are now permitting, thousands of young Ontario farmers, the cream of our Agricultural people, to leave their own Province for the West, while, by your inertia, you show you are not cognizant of the advantages of continued residence in this Province if full advantage is taken of the opportunities which open in response to intelligent effort."

The independent Conservative paper *"The Toronto World"* on February 14th, 1914, referring to the Liberal proposal for a Commission, said that the Government would be well advised to pay attention to it because Ontario is in need, and in bad need of something being done to rescue the agricultural interests of the country from the rut into which they have fallen, and which grows deeper every year. Even the *"Mail and Empire"* (Conservatives) confessed that the Department was lax in its administration. The following is an extract from the *"Mail"* of July 15th, 1913:—"It is true that the agricultural Department has not kept pace with the advance in other branches of industry."

It is unfortunately true that the Department of Agriculture almost ceased to operate during Mr. Duff's regime. Upon his decease things went from bad to worse through the Government's temporizing with a situation which demanded revolutionary changes and drastic reform that it did not receive.

Ever since the Conservative Party came into power in 1915 and particularly for the last five years, the Agricultural interests of the Province have been woefully neglected. The already overburdened Prime Minister, instead of appointing a practical farmer as Minister of Agriculture—a farmer with breadth of view and qualities of leadership—himself took charge of the Department and undertook to teach the farmers what he did not know about Agriculture, with the serious results to be expected. He had to be re-inforced by a Commissioner of Agriculture and an Assistant Commissioner, in addition to the Deputy Minister and Assistant Deputy already in the Department, but only caused increased dissatisfaction among the farmers of the Province.

The salaries paid to these particular gentlemen, as appears by the last edition of the Public Accounts, were as follows:—

G. C. Creelman as Commissioner, in addition to his salary as President of the Guelph Agricultural College $1,700.00
G. C. Creelman, President of Guelph Agricultural College, $3,000.00, total of 4,700.00
J. R. Miller, Assistant Commissioner 2,500.00
W. B. Roadhouse, Deputy Minister 3,450.00
C. F. Bailey, Assistant Deputy Minister 3,000.00

The Liberals protested that President Creelman could handle only one job at a time, but the Government persisted in its course of neglecting to provide a Minister to look after its Agricultural interests on account of its fear of a reverse at the polls, and endeavoured to hoodwink the farming community into thinking their interests were receiving attention by paying Mr. Creelman an additional $1,700.00 a year for acting where either he must neglect his work as President of the College or hold down his position as Commissioner to make it appear that the Government was doing something for Agriculture.

On account of the fact that the Government appeared afraid to open a constituency the Liberals offered to allow any Minister of Agriculture chosen by the Government to be elected without a contest at the bye-election which would be necessary. This offer was ignored by the Prime Minister.

The Government's Fear.

The bye-elections had not been going very well from the standpoint of the Government since the 1914 general election. Hamilton West in the general election gave the Government a majority of 1411, but in the bye-election consequent upon Hon. J. S. Hendrie accepting the office of Lieutenant-Governor of Ontario the majority was reduced to 36. In Dundas Sir James Whitney had a majority of 673. His successor managed to scrape in by 62 votes. Peel was the real black eye for the Government, when James R. Fallis who made a rake-off as intermediary between the Government and the public in the matter of the purchase of horses for the war, was obliged to resign. Peel had given Fallis a majority of 627 in the general election; Peel showed what it thought of profiteering by supporters of the Government, by defeating Fallis at the bye-election and electing a Liberal by a 305 majority. 1916 made the Government particularly nervous, North Perth was wrested from the Government. When the sitting member accepted the patronage of the Dominion Government the Liberals carried the seat by 549, as compared with the Government majority of 1117 in in the general election. Hartley Dewart, the present Liberal Leader in the Province defeated the Government wine and beer candidate in south-west Toronto by 551 votes. The late Attorney-General Foy held the seat by a majority of 3686.

During the session of 1917, when the Government sought to give effect to legislation making the various appointments in connection with the Department of Agriculture, (above referred to) the Liberals strongly opposed the measure and introduced an Amendment upon the second reading of the Bill to give it a six months hoist.

The Liberal Amendment was worded as follows:—

"Mr. Parliament moved in Amendment, seconded by Mr. Grieve.

"That all the words of the Motion after the first word 'that' be struck out and the following substituted therefor:—

"In the opinion of this House, the conditions created by the war make increasingly important the demand for efficient leadership and effective administration in the Department of Agriculture, and that the present urgent need is the appointment of a Minister of Agriculture to succeed the late the Honourable Mr. Duff, who is able to devote his whole time to the work of the Department, and who by practical training and experience is able to give leadership in Agricultural matters; and the appointment of a Deputy Minister, who by reason of his technical and practical knowledge of Agriculture, in this Province, is fitted to fill this most important post, and that therefore, the said Bill be not now read the second time, but be read the second time on this day six months."

The Government, however, voted down the Amendment and the Bill was eventually passed.

A Commission Demanded.

Both in the 1911 and 1914 election campaign the Liberals advocated on the platform a thorough investigation by a non-partizan Commission of the whole of the rural problem of Ontario, the establishment of suitable schools of Agriculture, increased attention to Agriculture in rural schools. They also favored demonstration farms throughout the Province, and the development of co-operative methods.

The resolution voted down by the Government during the session 1914 was as follows:—

"That in view of the serious decline in our rural population, as disclosed in our last decennial census, accompanied by a decline in the strength and vitality of the rural school and the rural church in many sections of the Province, and in the view of the general scarcity of farm labor throughout Ontario, which for some years past has caused grave concern to the farmers of the Province and contributed to a material diminution in the Agricultural production of the Province, this House is of the opinion that a non-partizan Commission of practical men should be appointed to inquire into the conditions of agriculture and of rural life in the Province, and report to this House the facts with their recommendations as to steps which can and should be taken to remedy or improve existing conditions."

In the year 1880 very fine results were obtained as the result of a similar investigation by the Mowat administration at that time. In that year a Commission of representative and practical men, interested in the problem of Agriculture was appointed to study the Agricultural condition of the Province of Ontario. This Commission made a most thorough and comprehensive investigation and presented its conclusions to the Legislature in the year 1881. The work of this Commission marked a new era in the Agricultural development of the Province. In order to make provision for more adequate attention toward supervision of the great work of Agriculture in the Province, Sir Oliver Mowat introduced a Bill in the year 1888, for the appointment of a Minister of Agriculture (this was opposed by the Conservative Opposition). The Government, notwithstanding opposition went ahead, and the Department was created, and under Hon. John Dryden great constructive measures were introduced and carried forward for improving the condition of Agriculture in the Province.

In addition to the motion already referred to, calling for a non-partizan Commission, which the Liberals presented in 1914, a further resolution was introduced in 1915, as follows:—"That in view of the serious decline in our rural population, accompanied by a marked falling off in food production, in the face of Ontario's unsurpassed agricultural possibilities and millions of acres of unoccupied agricultural land, this House is of the opinion that a great advance in the agricultural policy of the Government is one of the most urgent and vital needs of Ontario to-day, such policy to include:

"(1) Making more available to rural communities the scientific and technical knowledge taught in our agricultural college by the establishment of agricultural schools and demonstration farms throughout the Province; (2) The inauguration of an effective system of rural credits; (3) The development of co-operative effort in buying and selling; (4) Financial assistance by way of loans at a low rate of interest, on the security of land and improvements, to assist desirable settlers in establishing themselves in the newer parts of the Province, and to enable farmers in the older parts of the Province to improve and increase the productivity of their lands."

The Government moved an amendment to this motion expressing satisfaction with the soundness and stability of agriculture. The Liberals proposed a further amendment that "this House regrets that the Government does not propose any radical advance in its agricultural policy to meet the urgent situation now confronting us." The Government voted down the Liberals proposals.

What Mr. Marshall (Liberal Member for Lincoln), said in introducing his motion.

"My solution of the problem is in demonstration farms and associated with these, schools of agriculture. If you established institutions in connection with the demonstration farms to teach, you would be able to deal with the raising of live stock and other branches of agriculture. They could show how things should be done, and the demand in agriculture to-day is not so much for the men who can tell people how to do things, but the man who is able to do them himself.

There could be, in addition to that, a school for the girls that is urgently needed at the present time. It could teach work in the kitchen, cooking, sewing, sanitation and hygiene."

The Province of Ontario was being urged by the Government to produce more food. The Government made no attempt to formulate a policy in order to open up the huge tracts of unoccupied territory within the Province. Four concrete proposals were suggested by the Liberals in the above resolution but the Government ignored them and went on its way with a self-laudatory amendment.

In 1916 a similar motion was tendered to the House in which the Liberals emphasized the pressing problems which the war had created as the reason for Governmental action. In reply to this the Government merely congratulated the farmers on the response made for increased production.

The action of the Liberals of the House during the session of 1917 in opposing the multiple appointments in the Agricultural Department has already been commented upon. In 1918 protests were renewed. In 1919 a further effort was made to have a change effected. Mr. Parliament (Lib. Mem. for Prince Edward County) moved and was seconded by Mr. Bowman, (the U. F. O. Member for Manitoulin), as follows:—

"That this House recognizes the serious situation at present obtaining in the rural sections of the Province, due to the scarcity of labour for the farms. That this House also recognizes that the antebellum shortage of agricultural labour had been considerably aggravated by the last four years of war during which men flocked to the colors and were attracted to the cities by war-time wages, and that thereby a situation was created which threatened to curtail the volume of agricultural production, and that this situation still exists. That this House is therefore of the opinion that in order to discover the best means of encouraging a return to rural life in the Province of Ontario, the Government should appoint a non-partizan Commission (this Commission to include representatives of agriculture and labour), to inquire into the conditions which ordinarily account for the continuous diminution of rural population in the Province and to report to this House the facts and their recommendations as to the steps which should be taken to augment and maintain our rural population."

They both emphasized the difficulty in obtaining suitable farm help under present conditions; pointed out how the war had deprived Agriculture of many of its young men; discussed the need of increased agricultural production, which the Government had been advocating in a poster and literature campaign; and pleaded again for an inquiry into the conditions which might account for the continuous reduction of the rural population, so that the House might take steps to rectify the trouble when discovered. Mr. Parliament thought that great care should be taken in the matter of immigration. Efforts should be made to secure the very best class of people.

That the Government has neither the ability nor the willingness to do anything for agriculture is proved by the above facts taken from the official records of the House.

Rural Credits.

Discussing the question of Rural Credits during the course of a speech in the Legislature on April 11, 1919, Mr. Nelson Parliament, Liberal-Farmer Member for Prince Edward County, said:—

"I am glad to note that a member of the Legislature of the province of Manitoba has been in Toronto pointing out the benefits of rural credits in the province of Manitoba, and I hope that we will take a lesson from this man from the West and establish a real rural credit law in the province of Ontario, which I believe will be of immense benefit to the farmers of this province. I see no reason why for instance, we could not have farm loan banks or something of this nature in which the farmers could deposit their money to help one another."

Agricultural Schools.

Dealing with Agricultural schools, Mr. Parliament said:—
"We should have at least one Agricultural School in every county; and there should be more than ten or fifteen acres of land about it. We should have a real Demonstration Farm where every branch will be taken up. Instead of having one well qualified district representative there would then be 200 or 300 young persons well qualified in farm matters."

"I believe that the proper kind of schools in our rural communities with a Demonstration Farm and an Agricultural School situated thereon, with a winter term, would so broaden and fit them (the children) for their life's work that the outlay would not be considered. It would to my mind raise the standard of rural education so that it would not breed contempt for work but that it would ennoble a man's work and heighten his ability to perform it well, which is the proper ideal to strive for in moulding the mind of the young."

Decline in Rural Population.

The total rural population of Ontario in the year 1901, according to the official census, was 1,246,969. In the year 1911 the rural population was 1,194,785—a decrease of 52,184, persons. In the same time the total urban population had increased from 925,978 in the year 1901 to 1,328,489 in the year 1911, being an increase of 392,511 persons.

The census further shows that from 1901 to 1911 the rural population of Old Ontario declined by 97,124 and when the old and new parts are taken together the total decline is as above:—

The population of rural Ontario to-day is, moreover, 110,000 less than it was 40 years ago. The figures are as follows:—

Rural Population, Ontario 1871 1,306,405
Rural Population, Ontario 1911 1,194,785

Loss in 40 years 111,620

The City population, on the other hand, increased by 1,000,000 in the same 40 years, as follows:—

City Population, Ontario 1871 313,336
City Population, Ontario 1911 1,328,489

Increase in 40 years............ 1,015,043

It was in view of this serious decrease in the rural population and the consequent difficulty in obtaining farm labor that the Liberals agitated for the appointment of an investigating Commission.

We cannot go to a better place than Denmark to find out what Agricultural education has done. The area of Denmark is 15,000 sq. miles and the population 2,800,000 of whom 61 per cent. are on the land. Denmark has made rapid strides in agriculture and it has been through the schools that this notable advance has been made. In these agricultural schools the farmers are taught to make butter and other things. In 1904 Denmark exported in bacon, butter and eggs $68,000,000, and in 1912 $125,000,000, so that by encouraging a system of schools that suited the conditions in Denmark, they had been enabled to increase their output to a considerable degree. Co-operation has been more successful in Denmark than in almost any other country, and those who are in charge of education in Denmark state that the reason of such success was because the young farmers met together in these schools, had confidence in one another and worked in co-operation.

An analysis of the Public Accounts shows that the expenditures under the present Government for Agriculture have increased manifold without any corresponding result. No one complains about the expenditure of money for Agricultural and Educational purposes, but they do complain because of the lack of results. It is apparent that the fault lies with the present Government, which has refused to adopt an intelligent and enlightened policy with regard to Agriculture, and not with the Opposition, which has persistently urged an advanced policy upon the Government. The blame should be laid at the door of the present Government, where it belongs; but it is unfair that the present Agricultural movement should be directed against the Opposition, which has shown itself the consistent and steadfast friend of the farmer in the Province of Ontario.

Year after year the divisions of the Legislature show that the present members of the Opposition have stood together in support of the interests of Agriculture. They are entitled to the support of every farmer in the Province of Ontario. In contrast with the Liberal policy of Agricultural schools and Demonstration farms throughout the Province, the Government has a policy which has so far only developed one expensive Agricultural institute in Kempville, at the very door of the Hon. Mr. Ferguson, the Minister of Lands, Forests and Mines, at a point where it is probably least needed in the Province of Ontario, in such close proximity to the "Dominion Experimental Farm" near Ottawa. The cost of the Kempville institution could not be ascertained last session, except that a tender was accepted for $5,081 for the plumbing and heating.

It is simply a sop to the constituents of a Minister who is also spending fabulous sums in filling up the swamps between Ottawa and Prescott in an extensive scheme of highway construction. It is a pity that some of these expenditures could not be more evenly distributed.

The most recent evidence that the Government approves of the Liberal policy is found in the very specious pre-election bribe offered by the Premier to Essex in his speech at Leamington, when he said that it was the intention of the Government to start an Experimental Farm in this part of the Province to assist the peculiar needs of the type of farming carried out in the Western counties. The Premier explained that this part of the Province had been so progressive in an agricultural way that the people deserved much more support from the Government than they had received in the past.

If the Premier had any honest intention of creating such an institution when the House was in session why was it not referred to in the estimates? Why does he wait until his craft is in danger before he sends out this "S O S" to the people of Essex county? Neither they nor the people of the Province at large will be deceived by such tactics. It will be interesting to know whether in the course of his election tour of the Province he proposes to act in the role of an Agricultural Santa Claus in each of the ridings he visits.

GOVERNMENT HOUSE.

Before the Conservatives came into power they were very much opposed to expenditures in connection with a house for the Lieutenant-Governor and in 1895 moved the following resolution:—

"That in the opinion of this House the maintenance of Government House and the establishment connected therewith *at the expense of the Province,* should after the expiration of five years from the appointment or earlier termination of the term of office of His Honor, the present Lieutenant-Governor, be discontinued."

The Liberal Party never contended that an official house was not necessary, but that it should be maintained upon such a scale as was in keeping with the democratic spirit of the people of Ontario.

But in entire disregard of its partisan concern over-expenditure in this connection when in Opposition, the Conservative Party in power has erected a Government House in an entirely unsuitable location at a cost of over one million dollars. According to the official figures available, $1,098,104.08!

And it cost last year for repairs and maintenance $24,357.91, of which roughly $5,000 went in repairs and the rest in maintenance.

The following is a comparison of the estimated total cost as presented by the Government in reply to questions in the House in the three successive years, 1912, 1913, and 1914.

Estimated cost of building and site.. 1912 .. $400,000.00
Estimated cost of building and site.. 1913 .. 622,108.35
Estimated cost of building and site.. 1914 .. 875,015.65

The 1914 estimates are more than double those of 1912.

It has actually cost the country nearly three times the estimated cost.

In addition, the former Minister of Public Works made a special trip to Europe at a cost of $1,000 to the people of the Province, to examine the styles of furniture on the continent of Europe and in the castles of the Old Land.

The details of the expenditure, outside of maintenance charges, are as follows:—

Site .... $ 148,118.77
Improvements 182,596.23
Building 650,261.78
Other buildings 33,657.01
Furnishings 83,470.29

$1,098,104.08

Location.

Those who saw the present Government House site before Government House was located upon it wondered at this choice as a location for any important residence. Its chief merit at that time was its proximity to the residence of Sir William Meredith, the Government's Advisor-in-Chief. With high land all around it the Government chose a hollow overlooking the Don

Valley Brick Yards and Mackenzie & Mann's Railway Yards on the Don Flats; and a revetment wall had to be built at an expenditure of thousands of dollars, apparently to make sure that the lordly pile would not slip down into the valley below.

When one considers the closeness of the baronial pile to the residence of the Chief Justice of Ontario, one wonders why he did not protest against an extravagant expenditure unparalleled in the history of any Province. He could not have remembered the part that he took in the debates in the Ontario Legislature in 1880 when he was Leader of the Opposition. That was the time when the Mowat Government was contemplating the erection of the present Parliament Buildings in Queen's Park, Toronto, which stand as a monument to the energy, ability and conscientious honesty of the Hon. Christopher Findlay Fraser, the best Minister of Public Works the Province of Ontario ever had. Everyone who remembers the old Parliament Buildings on Front Street knows that they had outlived their usefulness and that the Government had to rent space in buildings nearby in order to accommodate the various departments of the Government with offices. The necessity for the new Parliament Buildings was great.

In the Speech from the Throne delivered by the Lieutenant-Governor at the opening of the Legislature in 1880, there appeared the following paragraph:—

"It appears to me therefore to be worthy of your very serious consideration, whether the erection of an edifice commensurate with the need of the public service and creditable to the Province should be longer delayed."

This roused the ire of Mr. W. R. Meredith, then Leader of the Opposition, who said:—

"On the proposition to erect new Parliament Buidings he was not in accord with the Government. . . . In East Toronto, which was being contested by the Leader of the Government (Mr. Mowat), a placard was published declaring that it was the intention of the Mowat Administration to expend a large sum of money in the erection of Parliament Buildings. . . . He denied that there was any special necessity for the erection of the new buildings. Historic memories surrounded the present building as the scene of action of some of the greatest Canadian statesmen, and of the passage of some of the greatest measures and these memories should not be disregarded. It was also said this House was unhealthy—that there were all sorts of gasses in it. In spite of its unhealthiness, however, the Hon. gentlemen in the Government who had been there for eight years still looked hale and hearty, and there seem to be plenty of people throughout the

Province who wanted to come there. It was a serious matter to take so large a sum out of the Treasury unnecessarily, and unless efforts were made to equalise the revenue and expenditure one of two results would happen—either a change in the present system or a withdrawal or reduction of our subsidies. It would be more for the benefit of the people, he thought, if the sum proposed to be expended for new Parliament Buildings were devoted to the erection of Training Schools for Teachers."

When Mr. Fraser, Minister of Public Works, moved the House into Committee of the Whole to consider the erection of new Parliament Buildings at a cost not to exceed $500,000, Mr. Meredith, speaking to the motion, said—"He believed that if the Government had told the country in the last election of their purpose in reference to the new buildings, they would not have received the support of the country. The Hon. gentlemen seemed to think that the present buildings were entirely unfit for the use of the Legislators. He ventured to say that the electors, if they had an opportunity to express an opinion, would not endorse that. They might say that if the buildings were needed and could be erected for a reasonable sum, it would not be a disadvantage. The position taken by the Hon. gentlemen that the present buildings were not convenient to one another and that they were isolated would go to the country and would mislead. The buildings were just as convenient as those now in use at Ottawa."

The contrast between the position of the Conservative Party with Mr. Meredith out of power and the position of the Conservative Party with Mr. Meredith as Chief Justice when in power is sufficiently striking to need no comment.

Liberals Urge Sale.

The size of this mansion for the Lieutenant-Governor and the cost of its upkeep cannot be defended by the Government. In 1915 the Liberals moved an amendment in Committee of Supply to sell the building and its contents for the best price obtainable and to purchase from the proceeds a more suitable site and to erect another building more in keeping with the democratic sentiment of the people of the Province. The amendment was as follows:—

> "That the resolution be not now concurred in, but, in view of the excessive and wasteful expenditure already made on the new Government House and the additional sums required to complete and furnish it on the present scale of expenditure, and of the heavy charge which will be made on the revenue of the Province for its maintenance, and in view of the unsuitability of the present site, be it

resolved that the new Government House be sold at the earliest practicable date for the best price obtainable therefor and from the proceeds thereof a suitable site be purchased and thereon erected a Government House in keeping with the democratic sentiment of the people of this province."

The Liberals pointed out that an Act had been passed by the Legislature expressly stating that a sufficient portion of the proceeds from the sale of the old Government House property should be set aside to constitute a fund the interest on which should provide for the maintenance, furnishing and repair of the new Government House and that "no other sums shall be appropriated by the Legislature annually for the maintenance or support of Government House." But it turned out that in the dying hours of the session, without notice to or knowledge of even the Leader of the Opposition, the Government had repealed this Act. It will be seen, however, that before the Act was repealed, in defiance of the law, the Government had proceeded with an enterprise that had wiped out entirely the amount received from the sale of the old property. It had to quietly repeal the Act to save its face.

Investigation showed that $800,000 had been derived from the sale of the old Government House and $60,000 more as a profit from the sale of the site first purchased for Government House, a total of $860,000. Yet the Government spent $1,100,000 overdrawing on capital account for its main expenditure and for the whole cost of maintenance, in reckless and extravagant disregard of all principles of decent and economic government.

Again in 1916 and 1917 the Liberals moved amendments recording their disapproval of this excessive and wasteful expenditure and the heavy charge made upon the revenues of the Province for maintenance, but the Government in every instance forced the estimates through the House by its partisan majority.

Expenditures Investigated.

The expenditures were investigated by the Opposition in the Public Accounts Committee during the session of 1917. There was not even the excuse for the tremendous increase in expenditure that there had been any material alteration in the plans. In answer to a question the Deputy Minister of Public Works stated "There were no material changes in construction." The grossness of the deception which was practised upon the House and upon the country is only too apparent.

Another point that developed was the fact that although enormous sums were expended, for example, $58,857.61 for tile mantels, decorating furniture and furnishings, tenders were not called for, and the major portion of the work went to the T. Eaton Co. Ltd.

The cost of the landscape work came to over $31,000, with an additional 10% commission of over $3,100 to the landscape artists.

The garage, Stable and Coachouse cost $14,637.00.

A cement ballustrade cost $7,404.00.

Fire-place fittings and grates came to $34,088.29.

An item of $684.00 for "cut flowers" turned out to be for bulbs and plants, but it was an example of the reckless way in which the accounts were made up and passed.

Amongst the items that were disclosed and which the Liberals condemned as wastefully extravagant were the following:—

Donegal rug for stateroom	$1,429.00
Donegal rug for Drawing-room	1,380.00
Donegal rug for living-room	898.00
Furniture for State Reception Room	3,597.00
One commode	700.00
60 Dining Room Chairs @ $24	1,440.00
Drawing-room furniture	2,004.00
8 prs. rose silk curtains	800.00
4 prs. green silk curtains	428.00
Curtains for ballroom	448.00
2 writing room curtains	190.00
Brass poles and fittings	1,234.00
State reception room table	310.00
Screens and other articles, including 2 Elizabethan hall tables @ $150	499.00
Rugs and tapestry	2,405.00
Oriental rugs for palm-room	1,165.00
Bedroom suite—the Duke	1,589.00

In the session of 1918 a further investigation in the Public Accounts Committee showed that 976 tons of coal costing $4,608.00 were purchased for the use of Government House during the preceding winter to heat this cold and costly castle, at a time when the coal famine and suffering were most acute in the Province.

The Government attempted to explain away this colossal expenditure by comparing Government House with the houses of American millionaires and others. The provincial architect considered there was nothing extravagant about the place, and yet it was shown that the main hall at Government House had marble floors, walls, pillasters, columns and balustrades.

Lightning Source UK Ltd.
Milton Keynes UK
UKHW050308101218
333419UK00018BB/2202/P